Windjammer Parade

Hans Jürgen Hansen – Benno Wundshammer

Windjammer Parade

Foreword by
Lieutenant Colonel The Lord Burnham

A Studio Book
The Viking Press · New York

Windjammerparade
© Gerhard Stalling Verlag, Oldenburg/Hamburg 1972
English language translation and Foreword Copyright © 1973 by Ian Allan Ltd.
All rights reserved
Published in 1973 by The Viking Press, Inc.
625 Madison Avenue, New York, N.Y. 10022
Published simultaneously in Canada by
The Macmillan Company of Canada Limited
SBN 670-77153-8
Library of Congress catalog card number: 73-6074
Printed and bound in West Germany
Cover photograph by Wolfgang-Peter Geller

On Sunday, September 3rd 1972, there sailed into Kiel some sixty-five sailing vessels, ranging in size from square-rigged ships of nearly 1800 tons Thames through schooners of 200–300 tons down to yachts of little over ten tons.

All the ships taking part in this remarkable parade had competed in races of some 500 or more miles. All were engaged in one way or another in the education of young men and women through the medium of the sea. Some, ranging from the great *Gorch Fock* from Germany and the *Eagle* from the USA down to the little yachts from the British Royal Naval College, represented their national armed services. These services have accepted that, even in an age of electronic navigation and sophisticated weapons, a basic knowledge of seamanship is still of value to those who seek to serve their country at sea. Others, such as the Polish *Dar Pomorza,* the *Danmark* and the Norwegian *Christian Radich* prepare young men for a career in their national merchant navies, who equally take the view that more is required in the making of a modern seaman than an expert knowledge of engines and the intricacies of radar. The majority of the vessels taking part, however, carried young people who had no intention of making a career at sea.

Their crews came under the aegis of organisations and individuals who appreciate that modern education, while catering admirably for individual mental and physical skills, has not yet succeeded in teaching people how to live and work together, and to accept rational discipline for the common good. Such men and associations have come to the conclusion that to achieve this vital object it is essential to work in an environment which of its very nature must be taken seriously—and this has led them inevitably either to the mountains or to the sea.

The Sail Training Association added to these aims a desire to see young people of all nations mixing together in friendly competition in the interests of international understanding and good will. Accordingly in 1956 they organised the first of the international Sail Training Races, from Torbay to Lisbon, and such was its success that similar events have been run since that date in alternate years and with increasing numbers of competitors. Struck by the glamour of the square-rigged ships and remembering the great sea poems of John Masefield, the Press christened these events the "Tall Ships Races". This name caught on immediately and has remained with us even though the races now include quite small yachts. Provided that they

carry young crews and share the original ideals of the Sail Training Association they can participate.

Each race is followed by an "inshore regatta" in which the crews compete in such events as swimming, rowing races, tug-of-war and dinghy sailing. These add to the opportunities for meeting each other which the crews already find when their ships gather at the starting and finishing ports. However, in 1972 for the first time the Sail Training Association organised an exchange of crews between ships during the cruise from Sweden to Germany after the races. Nearly a quarter of the young people taking part were able to sail in other ships, and since sixteen nations were involved, the permutations were almost endless. It was thought that the Colombian ship *Gloria* (with young men from ten nations aboard) held the record, but other ships taking part in the exchange suggested that *Gloria* had an unfair advantage since her original crew was recruited from four different countries. Particularly welcome to their new hosts were the girls from Finland, France, The Netherlands, Poland, and the United Kingdom who also took part in the exchange.

The 1972 series of races consisted of two major races—from the Isle of Wight to the

5

Skaw (645 miles) and from Helsinki to Southern Sweden (493 miles) and a final race from Heligoland to Dover (330 miles) for those returning home in a westerly direction. After the first two races the competitors gathered in Malmo and from there they cruised on to Travemünde and eventually to Kiel to take part in Operation Sail 1972.

Without the wholehearted co-operation of the civic and harbour authorities in Cowes and Helsinki, Malmo, Travemünde, Kiel and Heligoland, such an event could never have been organised. Special mention should also be made of the welcome provided by the Hanseatic City of Lübeck, which, though able to berth only a few competitors, contributed greatly to the reception of the fleet in Germany. The religious service for all denominations in the St. Jakobi church in Lübeck, conducted in five languages, was one of the most moving ceremonies that I have ever attended and will long remain in the memory of all who were there. However, the initiative of the whole enterprise must rightly be credited to Captain Hans Engel, former captain of the *Gorch Fock,* and Chairman of the Committee of Operation Sail 1972, which was formed at his suggestion to link this great occasion with the sailing events of the Olympic Games taking place at Kiel. Indeed a distinguished German speaker referred to Operation Sail as "the little sister of Olympia, without the politics". It was an accolade of which we are very proud.

Since even the most worthy of voluntary undertakings cannot be launched without financial support, our thanks are also due to all those individuals and organisations who made possible the latest series of Tall Ships Races. It is particularly appropriate that the *Cutty Sark,* most beautiful of all surviving sailing ships, should be associated with these events through the generosity of Berry Bros and Rudd Ltd, the owners of Cutty Sark Scotch Whisky, without whose financial aid the races would not have been possible.

This book aims to show you, its reader, through magnificent photographs, a little of the beauty, the drama and the comradeship which an apparently out-dated method of sea travel can still bring to the modern world. I hope you will be able to appreciate something of what it has meant to those who have taken part.

London 1973   BURNHAM

Photographs

by Benno Wundshammer

with further pictures by
Beken of Cowes
A. Bromley-Martin
dpa-Bild
Wolfgang-Peter Geller
Zygmunt Grabowiecki
Hanseatische-Luftfoto-Gesellschaft mbH
Eveline Hansen
Henrik Kabat
Koninklijk institut voor de marine
Hans Joachim Kürtz
Lehtikuva Oy
Hannu Lindroos
Friedrich Magnussen
Marinstabens Pressavdelning
Bernd Schiller
Roger M. Smith
B. A. Stewart
Suomen Kuvapalvelu Oy
Osmo Thiel
du Vinage
Harry Wunstorf

Captions by Hans Jürgen Hansen

Operation Sail 1972

This long and carefully prepared enterprise began quietly on a foggy windless day in Cowes and ended in triumph at the "Olympic Regatta of Windjammers" in Kiel. These great sailing ships, the last now sailing the seas, are all training ships and the event was organised by British Sail Training Association to whom we must be grateful for this rare glimpse of the bygone age of sail.

Since 1956 the Sail Training Association has organised an "Operation Sail" every two years, with regattas for the training ships and contests for their crews. In 1972 this culminated in a parade in Kiel on the occasion of the Olympic Games. Two separate races were held: one from Cowes across the North Sea to The Skaw (the northernmost point of Denmark) and the other from Helsinki across the Baltic to Falsterbo (the southernmost point of Sweden). All ships then assembled in the Swedish port of Malmo and sailed in flotilla for Lübeck/Travemünde for the crew contests, and finally on to the Olympic Parade in Kiel.

A hazy mist hung over the water as the fleet of tall ships gathered in Cowes on the morning of August 16th 1972 leaving their anchorage in the harbour and the roadstead to take up their places for the start off Spithead.

Right: Only a feeble sun glimmers through the haze as the Polish full-rigged ship *Dar Pomorza* prepares to weigh anchor.

Above left: The American brigantine
Black Pearl and behind her *Dar Pomorza*
on the way to the start.
Above: View from the bowsprit of
L'Etoile, the topsail schooner from the
French Naval College, and her sister ship
La Belle Poule, before leaving for the
start.
Below far left: The German brigantine
Falado von Rhodos sets off for the start.
Centre: The British three-masted topsail
schooner *Sir Winston Churchill* on the
way to the start. In the background the
British *Captain Scott*.
Left: *Malcolm Miller* and *Sir Winston
Churchill*, the two British sister ships with
the Isle of Wight in the background.

Left: *Eagle*, the US Coast Guards' barque, and the American brigantine *Black Pearl* get under way for the start. Cannon from *HMS Brighton* gave the starting signal at noon for Class "A", the great square-riggers *Dar Pomorza*, *Eagle* and *Gorch Fock*; and at quarter-hour intervals for the three

groups of smaller sailing ships: the schooners, brigantines, ketches, yawls, cutters and sloops. A light wind sprang up and through the dispersing mist the English coast came slowly into view.
Top left: The newest British training ship, *Captain Scott*, not taking part in the race, sails past the field of starters.
Lower left: The Dutch bermudian ketch *Norseman*.
Above right: The Dutch gaff ketch *Jacomina* from Amsterdam. Right: The French topsail schooner *L'Etoile*.
Far right: The German brigantine *Falado von Rhodos*. In the background the French *La Belle Poule*.

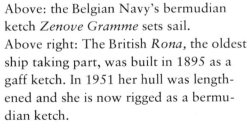

Above: the Belgian Navy's bermudian ketch *Zenove Gramme* sets sail.

Above right: The British *Rona,* the oldest ship taking part, was built in 1895 as a gaff ketch. In 1951 her hull was lengthened and she is now rigged as a bermudian ketch.

Right: *The Urania,* built in 1928 as a schooner-yacht and now rigged as a bermudian ketch, training ship of the Royal Dutch Navy, after the start.

Far right: *Gorch Fock,* still without sail, makes her way to the start. The Isle of Wight in the background.

Following pages: *Gorch Fock* sails before the wind through the English Channel.

Page 17: Hoisting sail before the start.

The rules of the "Tall Ships" races require that at least half of each ship's crew should still be under training, either as naval cadets or their civilian equivalent; but sail training is no longer an exclusively male preserve as girls are to be counted amongst many of the crews. *Sir Winston Churchill* for example was sailed entirely by girls, and she was to prove to be faster than her male-crewed sistership, *Malcolm Miller.*

The course from Spithead to The Skaw covers 650 nautical miles. As well as the three great square riggers, 39 other ships under 500 tons Thames made the crossing of the North Sea. On August 19th, the third day after the start, a storm broke and with wind strengths of up to Force 9 the voyage went faster than expected. Several small ships, however, had to seek shelter in Dutch coastal ports, or had to give up the race and run through the Kiel Canal to Malmo. Amongst the latter were the German *Seute Deern* and the British *Royalist.*

Below: All hands on deck to handle the ship during the storm.

The Italian bermudian yawl *Stella Polaris*, only 62 tons Thames, running before the gale with luck and skill, arrived off the Skaw lightship four days after the start. Overall, she was the fastest ship, forty minutes ahead of the Dutch *Urania. Dar Pomorza* was winner in Class "A", with *Gorch Fock* five minutes behind and *Eagle* third.

Following page: *Dar Pomorza* during the storm in the North Sea.

Pages 22–23: The beautiful *Gorch Fock.*

Below: In addition to those racing up from Cowes, other windjammers that were entered for the Baltic Regatta gathered in Helsinki.

As in Cowes, the morning of the start in the Gulf of Finland was also misty. At 1 pm on August 20th, a shot from a Finnish frigate gave the starting signal for the three participants in Class "A"; the Colombian barque *Gloria* and the two full rigged ships *Christian Radich* from Norway and the Danish *Danmark*. The first group in Class "B" (from 80 to 500 tons Thames) started at 1.30 pm and the second group (under 80 tons) at 1.45 pm.

Above: The gaff schooner *Te Vegas* from Panama, the largest ship in Class "B", and in the background the Danish fullrigged *Danmark*, before the start.

Right: The fullrigged ship *Christian Radich* from Oslo, under full sail.

Following page: Sunlight sparkles on the water as *Christian Radich* and *Danmark* stand silhouetted side by side as they wait for the start.

The gale in the Baltic proved even stronger than that in the North Sea, reaching Force 10 at times.

As well as the three large square-riggers there were more than 20 other ships on their way to Falsterbo leaving the southern coast of the Gulf of Finland and the Baltic coast to port and the Swedish islands of Gothland and Oland to starboard. In the strong north wind, they sailed the 493 mile stretch from Helsinki to Falsterbo under reduced sail. The Brazilian bermudian sloop *Santa Maria* had to give up and the Finnish staysail schooner *Marillisa* capsized near Gothland, fortunately without injury to the crew, and had to be towed into harbour.
Right: At the wheel of the gaff schooner *Falken* of the Swedish Navy during the passage through the storm in the Baltic.
Below right: *Gladan*, *Falken*'s sister ship.
Far right: *Falken* during the storm on course for Falsterbo.

Below: How *Falken* looked from *Gladan* during the voyage through the Baltic.
Left: On deck during the voyage.
On August 24th the West German Navy's bermudian sloop *Asta,* sailing in Class "B" was first over the finishing line at Falsterbo before the large ships in Class "A". Of these, *Christian Radich* was first, *Danmark* two hours behind her, and *Gloria* third.

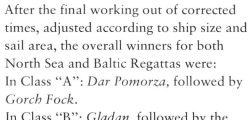

After the final working out of corrected times, adjusted according to ship size and sail area, the overall winners for both North Sea and Baltic Regattas were:
In Class "A": *Dar Pomorza*, followed by *Gorch Fock*.
In Class "B": *Gladan*, followed by the *Sir Winston Churchill*.
Left: The helmsman of *Gladan* during the storm.
The storm abated as the fleet of ships from both Regattas made its way to the common meeting place at Malmo.
Far left: *Dar Pomorza* off Malmo.
Below left: Cadets of *Malcolm Miller* at work on the bowsprit.
Below: On the deck of *Gladan*.

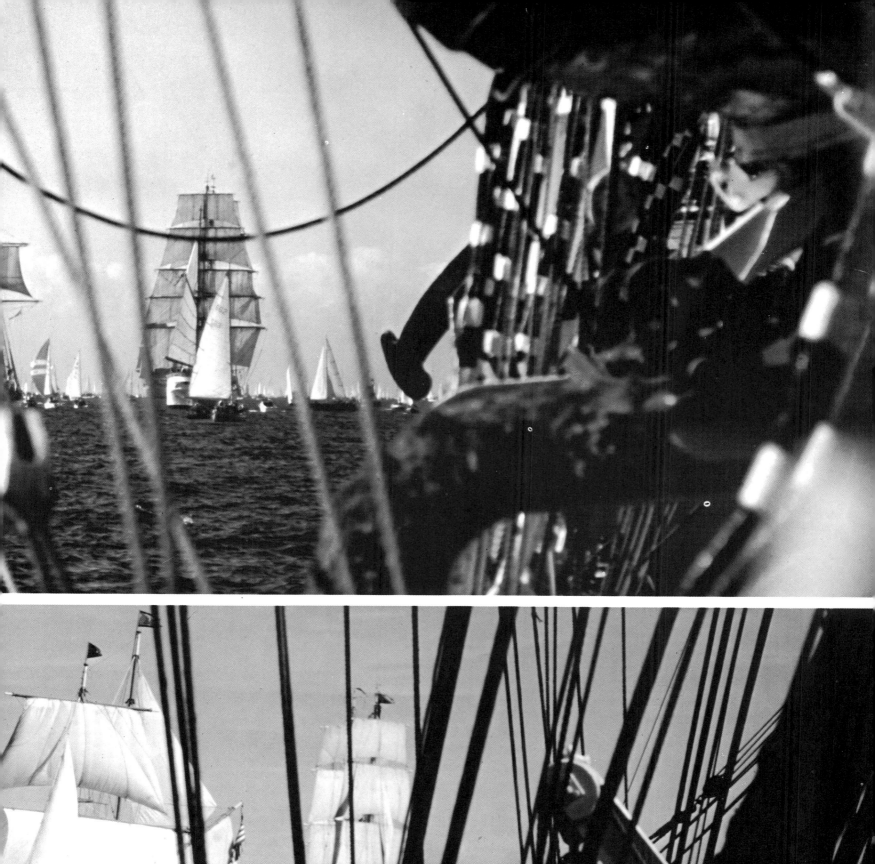

Previous two pages: The ships leave the harbour for Travemünde.
Right: Southward bound through The Sound. In front the American barque *Eagle;* in the background the coast of the Swedish Schonen peninsula.
After the race, the ships from all 17 countries rested in Malmo Harbour, repaired their storm damage, and were visited by thousands of sightseers from Malmo, Copenhagen and nearby areas of Sweden and Denmark.
Above top: The British brig *Royalist* with her carved prow alongside the pier at Malmo. Background right *Christian Radich* and *Danmark* are to be seen.

Above left: The German *Seute Deern, La Belle Poule* and *L'Etoile* lie side by side in the harbour at Malmo. In the foreground the American flag at the stern of *Black Pearl.*
Above centre: The Blue Ensign outlined against *Gorch Fock* lying at the pier.
Above right: The Finnish flag flies from the stern of *Susaleen.*

A favourable light north-easter was blowing as the flotilla sailed southwards making for Lübeck Bay and passing to the eastward of the islands of Zealand, Moën and Falster.
Left: Up the shrouds to work in the rigging.
Right: View from the foremast of the deck of *Gorch Fock*.
Following pages: *Gorch Fock* sailing for Travemünde.

Above left: Gulls accompany the ships,
flying high above the sails.
Above right: View of *Falken*'s foremast.
Below left: The girl deckhands of *Sir Winston Churchill*.
Below centre: At the helm of *Dar Pomorza*.
Left: A deck-officer of *Dar Pomorza* casts
a critical look at his crew working aloft.

Below left: The British bermudian cutter *Actaeon of Hamble.*
Below centre: The brigantine *Duenna* from Hamburg.
Below right: The American brigantine *Black Pearl* from Newport, Rhode Island.
At bottom: The three-masted topsail schooner *Sir Winston Churchill,* training ship of the British Sail Training Association from Bosham.
Right: View over the *Danmark*'s taffrail of *Christian Radich* and the flotilla of smaller sailing ships.

Above: Departure of the flotilla to the
south. In the foreground, the Colombian
Gloria.
Right: The American barque *Eagle*.
Far right: *L'Etoile* casting her reflection
on the sparkling water.

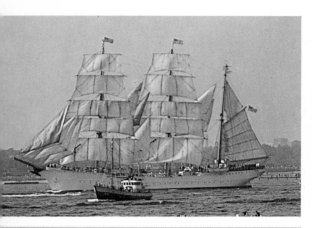

From top to bottom: The large square riggers *Eagle*, *Dar Pomorza* and *Gloria*.

Right: *Christian Radich*.
Left: *Danmark*.
Top: *Gorch Fock*.
Opposite page: During the voyage to Travemünde on the afternoon of August 27th. In the foreground is *La Belle Poule*. Following pages: Close-ups during the voyage. Left: *Gloria*. Right: *Eagle*.

Below: *Sir Winston Churchill* on the evening of August 27th.
Bottom: The Swedish schooners *Gladan* and *Falken* in the light of the evening sun.

Right: *Gladan* next morning silhouetted by the rising sun.
Following page: View through the shrouds of *Danmark* at *Royalist* sailing alongside.

The seaman's daily round goes ahead.
Far left: Hanging the washing out to dry.
Left: Deck scrubbing with bass brooms
and seawater.
Above: Two cadets from *Danmark*; one
Dane and his shipmate from Greenland.

Above right: Splicing a damaged rigging
cable.
Centre right, and right: All brasswork is
polished until it glitters, in readiness for
the coming visitors' days in Travemünde.

The flotilla of tall ships neared the German coast during the course of August 28th.

Above and right: *Dar Pomorza*. Favourable winds brought the first sails over the horizon to the eager watchers ashore during the afternoon. Before long all the ships had entered Travemünde Bay and dropped anchor.

Following pages:

Above: Furling the sails on board *Danmark*.

Below: *Malcolm Miller* in evening light.

During the night of August 28/29th more tall ships arrived and anchored in the Bay, then, at dawn, they all weighed anchor and began to enter the outer harbour. Thousands of people travelled during the night to Travemünde to watch the ships making their way into the mouth of the Trave in the morning sunlight.

Right: Behind the *Gratia* the sun appears over the horizon. Far right, above and below: The Polish three-masted staysail schooner *Zawisza Czarny* in the roadstead at Travemünde.

Below left: Just before entering the Trave.

Below right: The Dutch gaff cutter *MD3* at Travemünde.

Following pages:

Left: The French *La Belle Poule* still at anchor as the sun rises over the Mecklenburg coast.

Right: View from a porthole of *Gorch Fock*.

During the voyage from Malmo to Travemünde.
Far left and centre left: On board *Gorch Fock*.
Left: On board *Dar Pomorza*.
Above: View on to the deck of *Gorch Fock*.

Looking up the mainmast of *Danmark*,
during the voyage to Travemünde. 69

Far left: Yardarm view of the deck of
Gorch Fock.
Up the shrouds to furl the sails. Left: at
the crosstrees of *Dar Pomorza*. Above: on
the mainmast of *Gorch Fock*.   71

Below: *Gorch Fock* before entering the harbour at Travemünde.
Ship after ship sailed past the old lighthouse on the way into the Trave, watched by thousands of enthralled spectators. During the next five days, the sailing ships were open to the public. Almost 200,000 people are estimated to have visited the windjammers in Travemünde, and inspected *Gloria* and *Eagle*, which motored up the Trave as far as Lübeck.
Right: *Christian Radich, Dar Pomorza, Malcolm Miller* and *Sir Winston Churchill* at the mole in Travemünde.

After the contests between the crews, a
gala reception was given by the Hanseatic
town of Lübeck and prizes were awarded.
Then on September 2nd, the eve of the
grand parade, the ships set sail for Kiel.
Below: View from the mainmast on to the
deck of *Falken*.
Right: Topsail of *Falken*.

On course for the island of Fehmern. During the night all ships reached the Fehmern Belt, the strait between Fehmern Island and the Danish Island of Lolland. From there they set a northwesterly course, and finally arrived next morning in Kiel Bay from the northeast ready for the parade.

Below: View of the main and topmasts of *Danmark* with the helmsman in the background.

Right: The British brig *Royalist* sets sail.

The three barques on the way to the parade.
Above: *Eagle*, USA.
Centre: *Gorch Fock*, West Germany.
Right: *Gloria*, Colombia.
These three ships were all built to the same design, from the Blohm & Voss 1933 lines plan for the pre-war German Navy's training ship *Gorch Fock*, constructed in Hamburg, and which is now the training ship *Tovarischtsh* of the Russian Navy.

Eagle was also built by Blohm & Voss to the design for the old *Gorch Fock*, and was formerly the German training ship *Horst Wessel*. The present West German training ship *Gorch Fock* is an exact copy of her forerunner, built to the 1933 lines, and was constructed in 1950 by Blohm & Voss. The Colombian training ship *Gloria*, was built in a Spanish shipyard in Bilbao and also followed the design of the first *Gorch Fock*.

At 9 o'clock on the morning of September 3rd, the fleet of 67 ships stood 6 miles south east of the Kelds Nor beacon on the Danish island of Langeland, at the entrance to the Great Belt. It then followed a west-southwest course to a position 54 °N and 10 °E in Kiel Bay, 8 miles north-east of the Kiel lighthouse and almost exactly halfway between the Danish and German coasts–the chosen venue of the parade. Above and right: Proceeding to the parade.

In the meantime, in glorious summer weather, a mass migration towards Kiel was taking place. More than 25,000 cars packed the roads leading to the coast. At 10 o'clock some 30 tourist ships of various sizes with around 15,000 people on board, set sail for Kiel Bay to see the parade. At the head of this flotilla of visitors was the ship carrying the West German President, Dr Heinemann. The Munich and Kiel Olympic Games were taking place at the same time, and on this Sunday "Operation Sail" reached its climax in the great Windjammer Parade. The sun streamed down, but the wind was very light, as, with the help of their auxiliary motors, but under full sail, the ships took up their places in two rows before the fleet of tourist ships. More than a thousand smaller private boats, sailing yachts and numerous rowing and paddle boats were present.

Above: In rather hazy weather, accompanied by more than a thousand small boats, the windjammers sail from the assembly point of the parade to Kiel Harbour.

Right: View from the rear of the flotilla as it nears Kiel Harbour. Leading is *Gorch Fock*, followed by *Eagle*, *Gloria* and *Danmark*.

Above: In line, *Dar Pomorza*, *Gorch Fock* and *Eagle* sail ahead as flagships.

Above left: *Eagle,* surrounded by a cluster of accompanying boats.
Above: *Danmark* enters the harbour.

Far left: View of the Flotilla from one of the passenger ships.
Left: *Eagle* (left), *Gorch Fock* (in background) and *Danmark* (in front) among the sailing ships entering the harbour.

87

Right: Overshadowed by the great square riggers the ships sail in close formation towards the harbour on this rather hazy afternoon. In front left, *Dar Pomorza,* behind almost hidden, *Gloria,* and right, *Gorch Fock,* with, behind her, *Eagle.* Following page: *Dar Pomorza* during the parade.

Left: *Gorch Fock* and *Dar Pomorza* (in background) entering the harbour.
Right: *Eagle* enters the harbour.
Following page: View from *Eagle* of the field of following ships. In the centre, *Gloria* followed by *Danmark*.

Left and above: In the afternoon sunshine
the ships enter the harbour at Kiel.

The flotilla sailing to the parade.

Above: View from the bowsprit of *Eagle*
of the groups of ships sailing ahead.

The procession of ships stopped and one by one, each furled its sails. Some made fast in the inner harbour by the Blücher Bridge, others moored out in Tirpitz-hafen.

Following page: The flags lie on the deck of *Eagle*, ready to be hoisted to fly gaily over the mastheads. To the left, *Gorch Fock* and to the right, *Bel Espoir*.

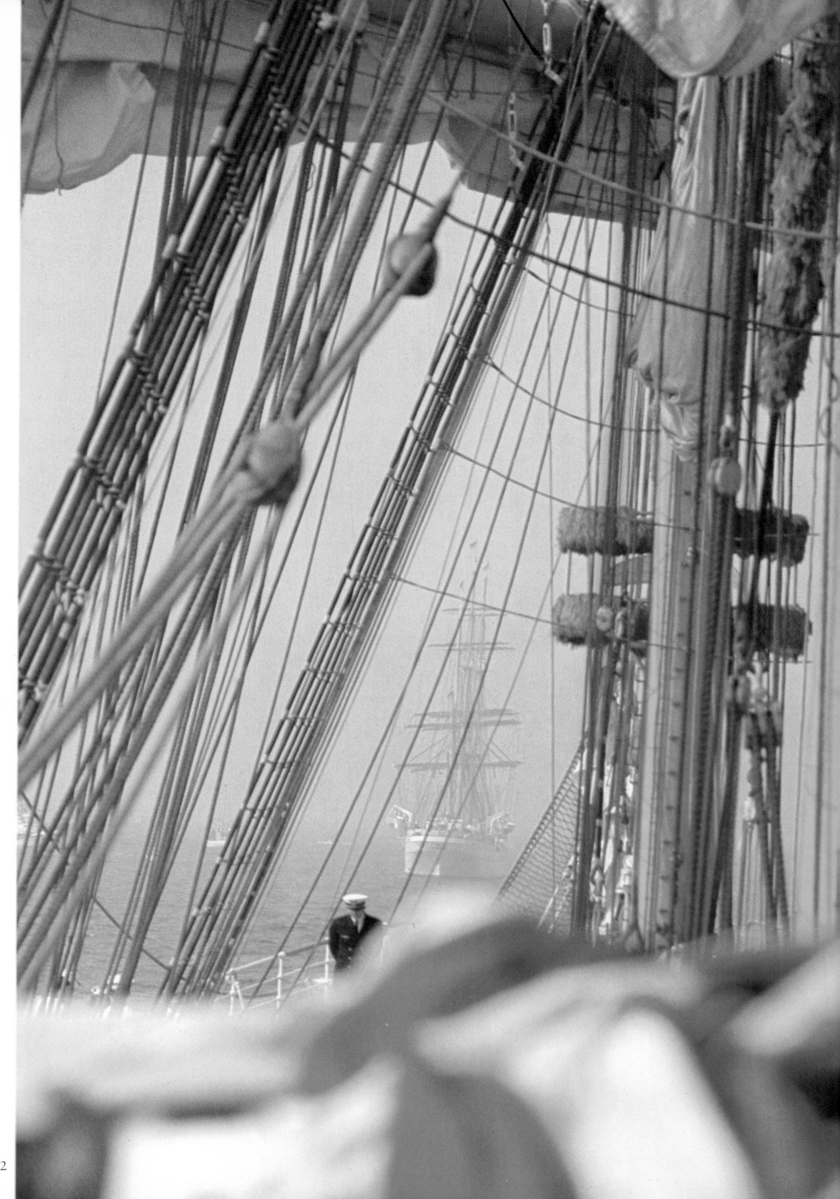

The big ships at the Blücher Mole. When
the Windjammer Parade came to an end,
more than half a million people had seen
it. Visualizing the time gone by when all
seagoing ships were under sail, many
agreed with Dr. Gustav Heinemann, President of West Germany, when he said:
"I have never seen anything more beautiful."

Ships taking part in the Windjammer Parade

**Great square riggers over 500 tons
Thames
(class "A")**

Christian Radich

Country: Norway
Owner: Ostlanders Skoleskib, Oslo
Captain: Asbjorn Espenak
Rig: full rigged ship
Hull colour: white
Year built: 1937
Builders: Frammaes Mek. Verkstad, Sandefjord
Tonnage: 773 tons Thames
Length over all: 72,50 m.; 237.9 ft.
Length between perpendiculars: 53,00 m.;
173.9 ft.
Beam: 9,70 m.; 31.8 ft.
Draft: 4,50 m.; 14.8 ft.
Sail area: 1234 qm.; 13283 sq. ft.
Auxiliary motor: 450HP
Permanent crew: 15, including 6 officers
Cadets: 88
Took part in: Helsinki–Falsterbo

Danmark

Country: Denmark
Owner: Direktoratet for Sofartsuddannelsen, Copenhagen
Captain: K. Groth
Rig: full rigged ship
Hull colour: white
Year Built: 1933
Builders: Nakskov Skibsvaerft, Nakskov
(Lolland)
Tonnage: 845 tons Thames
Length over all: 77,00 m.; 252.6 ft.
Length between perpendiculars: 54,50 m.;
178.8 ft.
Beam: 10,00 m.; 32.8 ft.
Draft: 4,20 m.; 13.8 ft.
Sail area: 1636 qm.; 17610 sq. ft.
Auxiliary motor: 486HP
Permanent crew: 16, including 6 officers
Cadets: 80
Took part in: Helsinki–Falsterbo

Dar Pomorza

ex Pomorze, ex Colbert, ex Prinzess Eitel
Friedrich
Country: Poland
Owner: Wyzsza Szkola Morska, Gdingen
Captain: Kazimierz Jurkiewicz
Rig: full rigged ship
Hull colour: white
Year built: 1910
Builders: Blohm & Voss, Hamburg
Tonnage: 1784 tons Thames
Length over all: 91,00 m.; 298.6 ft.
Length between perpendiculars: 72,60 m.;
238.2 ft.
Beam: 12,60 m.; 41.3 ft.
Draft: 5.70 m.; 18.7 ft.
Sail area: 1900 qm.; 20451 sq. ft.
Auxiliary motor: 430HP
Permanent crew: 39, including 12 officers
Cadets: 150
Took part in: Spithead–The Skaw

Eagle

Country: U.S.A.
Owners: United States Coast Guards,
New London, Connecticut
Captain:
Rig: barque
Hull colour: white
Year built: 1936
Builders: Blohm & Voss, Hamburg
Tonnage: 1561 tons Thames
Length over all: 89,70 m.; 294.3 ft.
Length between perpendiculars: 70,20 m.;
230.3 ft.
Beam: 11,90 m.; 39.04 ft.
Draft: 5,20 m.; 17.1 ft.
Sail area: 1983 qm.; 21345 sq. ft.
Auxiliary motor: 750HP
Permanent crew: 65, including 15 officers
Cadets: 110
Took part in: Spithead–The Skaw

Gloria

Country: Colombia
Owner: Armada Nacional de Colombia,
Cartagena
Captain: Guillermo P. Uribe
Rig: barque
Hull colour: white
Year built: 1968
Builders: Astilleros y Talleres Celaya S.A.,
Bilbao, Spain
Tonnage: 1300 tons Thames

Length over all: 76,00 m.; 249.3 ft.
Length between perpendiculars: 64,60 m.;
211.9 ft.
Beam: 10,60 m.; 34.8 ft.
Draft: 4,85 m.; 15.9 ft.
Sail area: 1400 qm.; 15069 sq. ft.
Auxiliary motor: 530HP
Permanent crew: 50, including 9 officers
Cadets: 60
Took part in: Helsinki–Falsterbo

Gorch Fock

Country: West Germany
Owner: West German Navy, Kiel
Captain: Ernst von Witzendorff
Rig: barque
Colour of hull: white
Year built: 1958
Builders: Blohm & Voss, Hamburg
Tonnage: 1727 tons Thames
Length over all: 89,30 m.; 293 ft.
Length between perpendiculars: 70,20 m.;
230.3 ft.
Beam: 12,00 m.; 39.4 ft.
Draft: 5,00 m.; 16.4 ft.
Sail area: 1952 qm.; 21011 sq. ft.
Auxiliary motor: 800HP
Permanent crew 78, including 14 officers
Cadets: 144
Took part in: Spithead–The Skaw

Schooners and training yachts from 30 ft. water line length up to 500 tons Thames (class "B")

Actaeon

Country: Great Britain
Owner: Lt. T. J. Playle, R. N. R., London
Captain: Lt. T. J. Playle, R. N. R.
Rig: Bermudian cutter
Colour of hull: blue
Tonnage: 34 tons Thames
Length over all: 16,09 m.; 52.8 ft.
Length of hull: 16,09 m.; 52.8 ft.
Beam: 4,27 m.; 14 ft.
Draft: 2,53 m.; 8.3 ft.
Permanent crew: 5, including 4 officers
Cadets: 9
Took part in: Spithead–The Skaw
106 Sail number: 120

Asgard

Country: Ireland
Owner: Ministry of Finance, Dublin
Captain: G. F. Healy
Rig: gaff ketch
Colour of hull: white
Year built: 1905
Builders: Colin Archers Vaerft, Rekevik
near Larvik, Norway
Designer: Colin Archer
Tonnage: 28 tons Thames
Length over all: 18,10 m.; 59.4 ft.
Length of keel: 15,45 m.; 50.7 ft.
Beam: 3,96 m.; 13 ft.
Draft: 2,15 m.; 7 ft.
Permanent crew: 3 officers
Cadets: 10
Took part in: Spithead–The Skaw
Sail number:

Asta

Country: West Germany
Owner: West German Navy, Flensburg-
Murwik
Captain: Jan-Eike Wolf
Rig: Bermuda sloop
Colour of hull: white
Tonnage: 28 tons Thames
Length over all: 16,30 m.; 53.5 ft.
Length of hull: 16,30 m.; 53.5 ft.
Beam: 3,81 m.; 12.5 ft.
Draft: 2,34 m.; 7.7 ft.
Permanent crew: 4 officers
Cadets: 5
Took part in: Helsinki–Falsterbo
Sail number G 785

Astral

Country: Dutch Antilles
Owner: Cornelius C. Vanderstar, New-
port Beach (California)
Captain: Cornelius C. Vanderstar
Rig: Bermudian ketch
Colour of hull: white
Year built: 1970
Builders: Krogerwerft, Rendsburg
Tonnage: 195 tons Thames
Length over all: 30,05 m.; 98.6 ft.
Length of hull: 30,05 m.; 98.6 ft.
Beam: 7,40 m.; 24.3 ft.
Draft: 2,00 m.; 6.6 ft.
Permanent Crew: 6, including 2 officers
Cadets: 6
Took part in: Spithead–The Skaw
Sail number: TS
                HA 24

Bel Espoir II
ex Prince Louis II, ex Peder Most, ex Nette S.

Country: France
Owner: Les Amis De Jeudi Dimanche,
Paris
Rig: three-masted gaff schooner
Colour of hull: black
Year built: 1944
Builder: J. Ring-Andersen, Svendborg
Tonnage: 189 BRT, 79,75 NRT
Overall length: 36,50 m.; 119.8 ft.
Length of hull: 27,40 m.; 89.9 ft.
Beam: 7,00 m.; 23 ft.
Draft: 2,60 m.; 8.5 ft.
Sail area: 465 qm.; 5005 sq. ft.
Auxiliary motor: 170 HP
Permanent crew: 5, including 2 officers
Cadets: 24
Took part in: Spithead–The Skaw

Black Pearl

Country: U.S.A.
Owner: Barclay H. Warburton, Newport
(Rhode Island)
Rig: Brigantine
Colour of hull: black
Year built: 1951
Builder: C. Lincoln Vaughn-Yard, Wick-
ford (Rhode Island)
Tonnage: 41 tons Thames
Length over all: 20,11 m.; 66 ft.
Length of hull: 16,64 m.; 54.6 ft.
Beam: 4,51 m.; 14.8 ft.
Draft: 1,86 m.; 6.1 ft.
Sail Area: 185 qm.; 1991 sq. ft.
Auxiliary motor: 150HP
Permanent crew: 6, including 5 officers
Cadets: 8
Took part in: Spithead–The Skaw
Sail number: TS
                US 33

Capella

Country: Great Britain
Owner: Britannia Royal Naval College,
Dartmouth
Captain: R. Claren
Rig: Bermudian cutter
Colour of hull: blue
Year built: 1934
Tonnage: 24 tons Thames
Length over all: 15,42 m.; 50.6 ft.
Length of hull: 15,42 m.; 50.6 ft.
Beam: 3,53 m.; 11.6 ft.
Draft: 2,31 m.; 7.6 ft.
Sail area: 85 qm.; 915 ft.
Permanent crew: 2 officers

Cadets: 8
Took part in: Spithead–The Skaw
Sail Number: 645

Dark Horse

Country: Great Britain
Owner: Lloyd's Bank Sailing Club, London
Captain: L. J. Jarvis
Rig: Bermudian sloop
Colour of hull: white
Tonnage: 17 tons Thames
Length over all: 13,25 m.; 43.5 ft.
Length of hull: 13,25 m.; 43.5 ft.
Beam: 3,47 m.; 11.4 ft.
Draft: 2,06 m.; 6.8 ft.
Permanent crew: 4 officers
Cadets: 4
Took part in: Spithead–The Skaw
Sail number: 2931

De Bonkel

Country: Holland
Owner: Dr. H. Kluvers
Captain: Dr. H. Kluvers
Rig: gaffsloop
Colour of hull: white
Year built: 1929
Designer: Ary de Boer, De Lemmer
Tonnage: 88 tons Thames
Length over all: 24,34 m.; 79.9 ft.
Length of hull: 24,34 m.; 79.9 ft.
Beam: 5,76 m.; 18.9 ft.
Draft: 1,49 m.; 4.9 ft.
Permanent crew: 2 officers
Cadets: 12
Took part in: Spithead–The Skaw
Sail number: $\frac{TS}{H\ 25}$

Duenna ex Sid, Will and Harry

Country: West Germany
Owner: Verlag Chronik der Seefahrt, Norderstedt
Captain: Egon Heinemann
Rig: Brigantine
Colour of hull: light blue over white
Year built: 1903
Builders: Aldous Bros., Brightlingsea (Essex)
Tonnage: 22 tons Thames
Length over all: 18,86 m.; 61.9 ft.
Length of hull: 14,60 m.; 48 ft.
Beam: 3,53 m.; 11.6 ft.
Draft: 1,80 m.; 6 ft.
Sail area: 150 qm.; 1615 sq. ft.

Auxiliary motor: 48 HP
Permanent crew: 5 officers
Cadets: 5
Took part in: Helsinki–Falsterbo
Sail number: $\frac{TS}{G\ 14}$

Falado von Rhodos

Country: West Germany
Owner: Dr. Herbert Horhager, Munich
Captain: Dr. Herbert Horhager
Rig: Brigantine
Colour of hull: red
Year built: 1968
Tonnage: 44 tons Thames
Length over all: 20,42 m.; 67 ft.
Length of hull: 14,99 m.; 49.2 ft.
Draft: 2,25 m.; 7.4 ft.
Permanent crew: 3 officers
Cadets: 7
Took part in: Spithead–The Skaw
Sail number: $\frac{TS}{G\ 19}$

Falken

Country: Sweden
Owner: Royal Swedish Navy, Karlskrona
Captain: Lt. Klas Oquist
Rig: two-masted gaff schooner
Colour of hull: white
Year built: 1946
Builders: Naval Shipyard, Stockholm
Tonnage: 232 tons Thames
Length over all: 39,62 m.; 130.00 ft.
Length of hull: 34,28 m.; 112.5 ft.
Beam: 7,20 m.; 23.6 ft.
Draft: 4,20 m.; 13.8 ft.
Sail area: 519 qm.; 5586 sq. ft.
Auxiliary motor: 128 HP
Permanent crew: 7, including 4 officers
Cadets: 30
Took part in: Helsinki–Falsterbo
Sail number: S 02

Galahad

Country: Great Britain
Owner: Royal Naval Engineering College, Plymouth
Captain: Sub-Lt. T. J. Lough, R.N.
Rig: Bermuda sloop
Colour of hull: green
Year built: 1961
Builders: Morgan-Giles, Ltd., Teignmouth, Devon
Designer: Morgan-Giles
Tonnage: 13 tons Thames
Length over all: 13,07 m.; 42.9 ft.
Length of hull: 13,07 m.; 42.9 ft.

Beam: 2,89 m.; 9.5 ft.
Draft: 2,10 m.; 6.9 ft.
Permanent crew: 2 officers
Cadets: 5
Took part in: Spithead–The Skaw
Sail number: 1775

Gawaine

Country: Great Britain
Owner: Royal Naval Engineering College, Plymouth
Captain: Sub.-Lt. W. Rosier, R.N.
Rig: Bermudian sloop
Colour of hull: brown
Year built: 1962
Builders: Morgan-Giles Ltd., Teignmouth, Devon
Tonnage: 13 tons Thames
Length over all: 13,07 m.; 42.9 ft.
Length of hull: 13,07 m.; 42.9 ft.
Beam: 2,89 m.; 9.5 ft.
Draft: 2,10 m.; 6.9 ft.
Permanent crew: 2 officers
Cadets: 5
Took part in: Spithead–The Skaw
Sail number: 1711

Gladan

Country: Sweden
Owner: Royal Swedish Navy, Karlskrona
Rig: two-masted gaff schooner
Colour of hull: white
Year built: 1947
Builder: Naval Shipyard, Stockholm
Tonnage: 232 tons Thames
Length over all: 39,62 m.; 130 ft.
Length of hull: 34,28 m.; 112.4 ft.
Beam: 7,20 m.; 23.6 ft.
Draft: 4,20 m.; 13.8 ft.
Sail area: 519 qm.; 5586 sq. ft.
Auxiliary motor: 128 HP
Permanent crew: 7, including 4 officers
Cadets: 30
Took part in: Helsinki–Falsterbo
Sail number: S 01

Glenan

Country: France
Owner: Centre Nautique des Glenans, Paris
Captain: J.-C. Gobert
Rig: Bermudian cutter
Colour of hull: blue
Tonnage: 14 tons Thames

107

Length over all: 13,37 m.; 43.9 ft.
Length of hull: 13,37 m.; 43.9 ft.
Beam: 3,22 m.; 10.6 ft.
Draft: 2,28 m.; 7.5 ft.
Permanent crew: 1 officer
Cadets: 8
Took part in: Spithead–The Skaw
Sail no: 2083

Gloria

Country: Finland
Rig: schooner
Took part in: Helsinki–Falsterbo

Gratia
ex Cinderella, ex Blue Shadow

Country: Sweden
Owner: Svenska Kryssarklubbens, Seglar-
skola, Goteborg
Captain: Sub.-Lt. Hendrik Wrede
Rig: schooner
Colour of hull: blue
Year built: 1900
Tonnage: 89 tons Thames
Length over all: 31,85 m.; 104.5 ft.
Length of hull: 28,22 m.; 92.6 ft.
Beam: 5,03 m.; 16.5 ft.
Draft: 2,80 m.; 9.2 ft.
Sail area: 318 qm.; 3423 sq. ft.
Auxiliary motor: 150 HP
Permanent crew: 7, including 3 officers
Cadets: 18
Took part in: Helsinki–Falsterbo
Sail number: 20

Gratitude

Country: Sweden
Owner: Svenska Kryssarklubbens, Seglar-
skola, Goteborg
Captain: Master Mariner Kjell Wollter
Rig: gaff ketch
Colour of hull: blue
Year built: 1908
Tonnage: 103 tons Thames
Length over all: 29,10 m.; 95.5 ft.
Length of hull: 23,01 m.; 75.5 ft.
Beam: 5,91 m.; 19.4 ft.
Draft: 2,71 m.; 8.9 ft.
Sail area: 340 qm.; 3660 sq. ft.
Auxiliary motor: 80 HP
Permanent crew: 7, including 3 officers
Cadets: 20
Took part in: Helsinki–Falsterbo
Sail number: 4

Grietje

Country: Holland
Owner: Erik Hoffmann, Bussum
Captain: Erik Hoffmann
Rig: gaff ketch
Tonnage: 45 tons Thames
Length over all: 21,15 m.; 70.5 ft.
Length of hull: 17,16 m.; 56.3 ft.
Beam: 4,81 m.; 15.8 ft.
Draft: 2,92 m.; 9.6 ft.
Permanent crew: 5 officers
Cadets: 5
Took part in: Spithead–The Skaw

Gryphis

Country: Great Britain
Owner: Britannia Royal Naval College,
Dartmouth
Captain: Lt. Cdr. J. Oliver
Rig: Bermudian sloop
Colour of hull: white
Year built: 1959
Builders: Morgan-Giles, Ltd., Teign-
mouth, Devon
Tonnage: 13 tons Thames
Length over all: 13,07 m.; 42.9 ft.
Length of hull: 13,07 m.; 42.9 ft.
Beam: 2,89 m.; 9.5 ft.
Draft: 2,04 m.; 6.7 ft.
Permanent crew: 2 officers
Cadets: 5
Took part in: Spithead–The Skaw
Sail number: 1124

Hamburg VII

Country: West Germany
Owner: Norddeutscher Regattaverein,
Hamburg
Captain: Gunther K. Reher
Rig: Bermudian yawl
Colour of hull: white
Tonnage: 29 tons Thames
Length over all: 16,61 m.; 54.5 ft.
Length of hull: 16,61 m.; 54.5 ft.
Beam: 3,96 m.; 13 ft.
Draft: 2,56 m.; 8.4 ft.
Permanent crew: 2 officers
Cadets: 9
Took part in: Spithead–The Skaw
Sail number: G 164

Hoshi

Country: Great Britain
Owner: The Island Cruising Club, Sal-
combe, Devon
Captain: Lt. Cdr. T. C. J. Martins, R.N.
Rig: gaff schooner
Colour of hull: green
Tonnage: 50 tons Thames
Length over all: 25,45 m.; 83.5 ft.
Length of hull: 21,90 m.; 71.9 ft.
Beam: 4,33 m.; 14.2 ft.
Draft: 2,37 m.; 7.8 ft.
Permanent crew: 5 officers
Cadets: 8
Took part in: Spithead–The Skaw
Sail number: 1887

Jacomina

Country: Holland
Owner: Jan Derwig, Amsterdam
Captain: Jan Derwig
Rig: gaff ketch
Colour of hull: black
Year built: 1926
Tonnage: 66 tons Thames
Length over all: 19,14 m.; 62.8 ft.
Length of hull: 14,93 m.; 49 ft.
Beam: 5,49 m.; 18 ft.
Draft: 2,13 m.; 7 ft.
Permanent crew: 5, including 3 officers
Cadets: 5
Took part in: Spithead The Skaw
Sail number: $\dfrac{\text{TS}}{\text{H 27}}$

Joanna of Foulness

Country: Great Britain
Owner: N. S. Heriot, Staplers, Great
Totham
Captain: N.S. Heriot
Rig: Brigantine
Colour of hull: blue
Year built: 1970
Builders: Frank Curtis & Pape Broth.,
Looe, Cornwall
Tonnage: 18 tons Thames
Length over all: 16,30 m.; 53.5 ft.
Length of hull: 13,10 m.; 43 ft.
Beam: 3,41 m.; 11.2 ft.
Permanent crew: 3 officers
Cadets: 3
Took part in: Spithead–The Skaw
Sail number: $\dfrac{\text{TS}}{\text{K 36}}$

La belle Poule

Country: France
Owner: Naval School, Brest
Captain: Lt. Daniel
Rig: topsail schooner
Colour of hull: white
Year built: 1932
Builder: Chantiers Naval de Normandie, Fecamp
Tonnage: 225 tons Thames
Length over all: 35,35 m.; 116 ft.
Length of hull: 30,26 m.; 99.3 ft.
Beam: 7,40 m.; 24.3 ft.
Draft: 3,50 m.; 11.5 ft.
Sail area: 424 qm.; 4564 sq. ft.
Auxiliary motor: 100 HP
Permanent crew: 18, including 3 officers
Cadets: 12
Took part in: Spithead–The Skaw
Sail Number: $\dfrac{TS}{F\ 30}$

La Goleta

Country: Great Britain
Owner: C. J. Lawrence, London
Captain: C.J. Lawrence
Rig: staysail schooner
Colour of hull: white
Tonnage: 30 tons Thames
Length over all: 19,35 m.; 63.5 ft.
Length of hull: 16,61 m.; 54.5 ft.
Beam: 3,78 m.; 12.4 ft.
Draft: 2,28 m.; 7.5 ft.
Permanent crew: 2 officers
Cadets: 4
Took part in: Spithead–The Skaw
Sail number: 204

Larvik

Country: Great Britain
Owner: Lt. Cdr. I. D. G. Graham, R.N., London
Captain: Lt. Cdr. Mark Miller, R.N.R.
Rig: gaff ketch
Colour of hull: blue
Designer: Colin Archer
Tonnage: 43 tons Thames
Length over all: 17.86 m.; 58.6 ft.
Length of hull: 14,23 m.; 46.7 ft.
Beam: 4,84 m.; 15.9 ft.
Draft: 2,31 m.; 7.6 ft.
Permanent Crew: 4, including 3 officers
Cadets: 8
Took part in: Spithead–The Skaw
Sail number: $\dfrac{TS}{K\ 5}$

Leopard

Country: Great Britain
Owner: Britannia Royal Naval College, Dartmouth
Captain: Lt. Cdr. J. G. Pangbourne, R.N.
Rig: Bermudian sloop
Colour of hull: white
Year built: 1959
Builder: Morgan-Giles Ltd., Teignmouth, Devon
Tonnage: 13 tons Thames
Length over all: 13,07 m.; 42.9 ft.
Length of hull: 13,07 m.; 42.9 ft.
Beam: 2,89 m.; 9.5 ft.
Draft: 2,04 m.; 6.7 ft.
Permanent crew: 2 officers
Cadets: 5
Took part in: Spithead–The Skaw
Sail number: 1125

L'etoile

Country: France
Owner: Ecole Navale, Brest
Captain: Lt. Richard
Rig: topsail schooner
Colour of hull: white
Year built: 1932
Builders: Chantiers Naval de Normandie, Fecamp
Tonnage: 225 tons Thames
Length over all: 35,35 m.; 116 ft.
Length of hull: 30,26 m.; 99.3 ft.
Beam: 7,40 m.; 24.3 ft.
Draft: 3,50 m.; 11.5 ft.
Sail area: 424 qm.; 4564 sq. ft.
Auxiliary motor: 100 HP
Permanent crew: 18, including 3 officers
Cadets: 12
Took part in: Spithead–The Skaw
Sail number: $\dfrac{TS}{F\ 31}$

Malcolm Miller

Country: Great Britain
Owner: The Sail Training Association, Bosham
Captain: Captain G. R. Shaw, D.S.C.
Rig: three-masted topsail schooner
Colour of hull: black
Year built: 1967
Builders: John Lewis & Sons Ltd., Aberdeen.
Designer: Camper & Nicholson Ltd., Naval Architects
Tonnage: 299 tons Thames
Length over all: 45,41 m.; 149 ft.
Length of hull: 41,14 m.; 135 ft.
Beam: 8,10 m.; 26.6 ft.
Draft: 4,73 m.; 15.6 ft.

Sail area: 817 qm.; 8794 sq. ft.
Auxiliary motor: 240 HP
Permanent crew: 11, including 8 officers
Cadets: 44
Took part in: Spithead–The Skaw
Sail number: $\dfrac{TS}{K\ 2}$

Marabu

Country: Great Britain
Owner: Royal Navy, Portsmouth
Captain: Lt. Cdr. A. Hardy, R.N.
Rig: Bermudian ketch
Colour of hull: blue
Year built: 1935
Tonnage: 26 tons Thames
Length over all: 17,46 m.; 57.3 ft.
Length of hull: 17,46 m.; 57.3 ft.
Beam: 3,47 m.; 11.4 ft.
Draft: 2,28 m.; 7.5 ft.
Permanent crew: 4 officers
Cadets: 5
Took part in: Spithead–The Skaw
Sail number: 625

Martlet

Country: Great Britain
Owner: Britannia Royal Naval College, Dartmouth
Captain: Lt. Cdr. H. White, R. N.
Rig: Bermudian sloop
Colour of hull: white
Year built: 1959
Builders: Morgan-Giles Ltd., Teignmouth, Devon
Tonnage: 13 tons Thames
Length over all: 13,07 m.; 42.9 ft.
Length of hull: 13,07 m.; 42.9 ft.
Beam: 2,89 m.; 9.5 ft.
Draft: 2,04 m.; 6.7 ft.
Permanent crew: 2 officers
Cadets: 5
Took part in: Spithead–The Skaw
Sail number: 1126

MD 3

Country: Holland
Owner: H. Hortensius, Marken
Captain: Dr. B. Kraal
Rig: gaff cutter
Colour of hull: green
Year built: 1897
Builder: F. Smit, Kinderdyk
Tonnage: 51 tons Thames
Length over all: 22,00 m.; 72.2 ft.
Length of hull: 17,31 m.; 56.8 ft.
Beam: 5,12 m.; 16.8 ft.
Draft: 1,22 m.; 4 ft.

Permanent crew: 7, including 2 officers
Cadets: 7
Sail number: $\frac{TS}{H\ 29}$

Meriliissa

Country: Finland
Owner: Heikki Herrala, Helsinki
Captain: Heikki Herrala
Rig: staysail schooner
Colour of hull: black
Tonnage: 49 tons Thames
Length over all: 19,84 m.; 65.1 ft.
Length of hull: 17,00 m.; 55.8 ft.
Beam: 4,75 m.; 15.6 ft.
Draft: 2,13 m.; 7 ft.
Permanent crew: 1 officer
Cadets: 8
Took part in: Helsinki–Falsterbo
Sail number: $\frac{TS}{L\ 41}$

Merisissi

Country: Finland
Owner: Turun Partio-Sissit Ry, Turku
Captain: Cpt. Pantti Ajanko
Rig: Bermudian ketch
Colour of hull: blue
Tonnage: 25 tons Thames
Length over all: 13,59 m.; 44.6 ft.
Length of hull: 12,10 m.; 39.7 ft.
Beam: 4,14 m.; 13.6 ft.
Draft: 1,79 m.; 5.9 ft.
Permanent crew: 5 officers
Cadets: 5
Took part in: Helsinki–Falsterbo
Sail number: 27

Merlin

Country: Great Britain
Owner: Royal Navy, Naval Air Command, Lee-On-Solent
Captain: P. O. T. Wilkinson
Rig: Bermudian sloop
Colour of hull: blue
Year built: 1938
Tonnage: 25 tons Thames
Length over all: 16,82 m.; 55.2 ft.
Length of hull: 16,82 m.; 55.2 ft.
Beam: 3,44 m.; 11.3 ft.
Draft: 2,59 m.; 8.5 ft.
Permanent crew: 4 officers
Cadets: 6
Took part in: Spithead–The Skaw
Sail number: 662

Norseman

Country: Holland
Owner: Watersport "Twellegea", Vitwelleringa near Sneek
Captain: H. J. Rolff
Rig: Bermuda ketch
Colour of hull: blue
Year built: 1972
Designer: S. van der Meer
Tonnage: 38 tons Thames
Length over all: 17,52 m.; 57.5 ft.
Length of hull: 15,85 m.; 52 ft.
Beam: 4,60 m.; 15.1 ft.
Draft: 2,13 m.; 7 ft.
Permanent crew: 7, including 2 officers
Cadets: 7
Took part in: Spithead–The Skaw
Sail number: $\frac{TS}{H\ 26}$

Pegasus

Country: Great Britain
Owner: Britannia Royal Naval College, Dartmouth
Captain: Midshipman R. E. Jones, R.N.
Rig: Bermudian sloop
Colour of hull: white
Year built: 1959
Builders: Morgan-Giles Ltd., Teignmouth, Devon
Tonnage: 13 tons Thames
Length over all: 13,07 m.; 42.9 ft.
Beam: 2,89 m.; 9.5 ft.
Draft: 2,04 m.; 6.7 ft.
Permanent crew: 2 officers
Cadets: 5
Took part in: Spithead–The Skaw
Sail number: 1123

Peter von Danzig

Country: West Germany
Owner: Akademischer Segler-Verein, Kiel.
Captain: Reinhard Laucht
Rig: Bermudian yawl
Colour of hull: white
Tonnage: 38 tons Thames
Length over all: 17,98 m.; 59 ft.
Length of hull: 17,98 m.; 59 ft.
Beam: 4,11 m.; 13.5 ft.
Draft: 2,53 m.; 8.3 ft.
Permanent crew: 3 officers
Cadets: 10
Took part in: Spithead–The Skaw
Sail number: G 77

Pirat

Country: Poland
Owner: Polskiklub Morski, Danzig
Captain: Bodeslaw Reymann
Rig: gaff cutter
Tonnage: 6 tons Thames
Length over all: 8,45 m.; 27.7 ft.
Length of hull: 7,28 m.; 23.9 ft.
Beam: 2,6 m.; 8.5 ft.
Draft: 1,70 m.; 5.6 ft.
Permanent crew: 1
Cadets: 5

Regina IV

Country: West Germany
Owner: Akademischer Segler-Verein, Kiel
Captain: Dr. Heino Friedericks
Rig: Bermudian cutter
Colour of hull: white
Tonnage: 26 tons Thames
Length over all: 14,81 m.; 48.6 ft.
Length of hull: 14,81 m.; 48.6 ft.
Beam: 3,87 m.; 12.7 ft.
Draft: 2,10 m.; 6.9 ft.
Permanent crew: 3 officers
Cadets: 5
Took part in: Helsinki–Falsterbo
Sail number: G 133

Rona

Country: Great Britain
Owner: The Rona Trust, Gosport
Captain: Lt. Col. J. E. Myatt, R.A.
Rig: Bermudian ketch
Colour of hull: white
Year built: 1895
Tonnage: 48 tons Thames
Length over all: 23,62 m.; 77.5 ft.
Length of hull: 23,62 m.; 77.5 ft.
Beam: 3,96 m.; 13 ft.
Draft: 2,89 m., 9.5 ft.
Permanent crew: 5 officers
Country: West Germany
Took part in: Spithead–The Skaw
Sail number: $\frac{TS}{K\ 9}$

Royalist

Country: Great Britain
Owner: Sea Cadet Corps, London
Captain: Cdr. John Wheeler, R.N.
Rig: brig
Colour of hull: black with white band
Year built: 1971
Tonnage: 110 tons Thames
Length over all: 28,07 m.; 92.1 ft.

Length of hull: 23,31 m.; 76.5 ft.
Beam: 5,94 m.; 19.5 ft.
Draft: 2,74 m.; 9 ft.
Sail area: 580 qm.; 6243 sq. ft.
Auxiliary motor: 400 HP
Permanent crew: 9
Cadets: 23
Took part in: Spithead–The Skaw
Sail number: TS / K 23

St. Barbara II

Country: Great Britain
Owner: The Royal Artillery Yacht Club, Dortmund
Captain: Major M. J. R. May, R.A.
Rig: Bermudian sloop
Colour of hull: red
Tonnage: 14 tons Thames
Length over all: 12,59 m.; 41.3 ft.
Length of hull: 12,59 m.; 41.3 ft.
Beam: 3,26 m.; 10.7 ft.
Draft: 1,98 m.; 6.5 ft.
Permanent crew: 3 officers
Cadets: 5
Took part in: Helsinki–Falsterbo
Sail number: 114

St. Barbara III

Country: Great Britain
Owner: The Royal Artillery Yacht Club, Salisbury
Captain: Major M. C. Brown, R.A.
Rig: Bermudian sloop
Colour of hull: blue
Year built: 1971
Builder: Camper & Nicholson Ltd., Gosport
Tonnage: 17 tons Thames
Length over all: 13,25 m.; 43.5 ft.
Length of hull: 13,25 m.; 43.5 ft.
Beam: 3,47 m.; 11.4 ft.
Draft: 2,13 m.; 7 ft.
Permanent crew: 3 officers
Cadets: 5
Took part in: Spithead–The Skaw
Sail number: 211

Ste. Anne VII

Country: France
Owner: Centre Nautique de Glenans, Paris
Captain: Daniel Gaudin
Rig: Bermudian sloop
Colour of hull: white
Tonnage: 10 tons Thames

Length over all: 11,28 m.; 37 ft.
Length of hull: 11,28 m.; 37 ft.
Beam: 2,95 m.; 9.7 ft.
Draft: 1,94 m.; 6.4 ft.
Permanent crew: 1 officer
Cadets: 7
Took part in: Spithead–The Skaw
Sail number: 2524

Sansibar II

Country: West Germany
Owner: Hochseesegelschule H. Schnelle, Hamburg
Captain: H. Schnelle
Rig: Bermudian yawl
Colour of hull: white
Tonnage: 16 tons Thames
Length over all: 12,65 m.; 41.5 ft.
Length of hull: 12,65 m.; 41.5 ft.
Beam: 3,29 m.; 10.8 ft.
Draft: 1,76 m.; 5.8 ft.
Permanent crew: 4, including 1 officer
Cadets: 6
Took part in: Helsinki–Falsterbo
Sail number: G 7/126

Santa Maria

Country: Brazil
Owner: Hans Viktor Howaldt, Jürgen Kiep
Captain: Cdr. Hans Viktor Howaldt
Rig: Bermudian sloop
Colour of hull: blue
Tonnage: 20 tons Thames
Length over all: 15,03 m.; 49.3 ft.
Permanent crew: 4, including 3 officers
Cadets: 4
Took part in: Helsinki–Falsterbo
Sail number: BL 162

Sea Laughter

Country: Great Britain
Owner: D. F. O. Russell, Cousley Wood, Wadhurst, Sussex
Captain: Lt. Cdr. H. F. M. Scott, R.N.R.
Rig: Bermudian ketch
Colour of hull: white
Tonnage: 43 tons Thames
Length over all: 18,59 m.; 61 ft.
Length of hull: 18,59 m.; 61 ft.
Beam: 4,39 m.; 14.4 ft.
Draft: 2,04 m.; 6.7 ft.
Permanent crew: 4, including 3 officers
Cadets: 4
Took part in: Helsinki–Falsterbo
Sail number: TS / K 32

Seute Deern
ex Noona Dan, ex Haver

Country: West Germany
Owner: Deutscher Schulschiff-Verein, Bremen
Captain: G. Ohlf
Rig: gaff ketch
Colour of hull: black
Year built: 1939
Builder: J. Ring-Andersen, Svendborg
Tonnage: 187 tons Thames
Length over all: 36,57 m.; 120 ft.
Length of hull: 29,99 m.; 98.4 ft.
Beam: 7,13 m.; 23.4 ft.
Draft: 3,35 m.; 11 ft.
Sail area: 275 qm.; 2960 sq. ft.
Auxiliary motor: 165 HP
Permanent crew: 12, including 8 officers
Cadets: 15
Took part in: Spithead–The Skaw

Sir Winston Churchill

Country: Great Britain
Owner: The Sail Training Association, Bosham
Captain: Cpt. C. P. R. Collis
Rig: three-masted topsail schooner
Colour of hull: black
Year built: 1965
Builder: Richard Dunston (Hessle) Ltd., Haven Shipyard, Hessle, Yorkshire.
Designer: Camper & Nicholson, Ltd., Naval Architects
Tonnage: 299 tons Thames
Length over all: 45,41 m.; 149 ft.
Length of hull: 41,14 m.; 135 ft.
Beam: 8,10 m.; 26.6 ft.
Draft: 4,73 m.; 15.5 ft.
Sail area: 817 qm.; 8794 sq. ft.
Auxiliary motor: 240 HP
Permanent crew: 11, including 8 officers
Cadets: 44
Took part in: Spithead–The Skaw
Sail number: TS / K 1

Stella Polaris

Country: Italy
Owner: Italian Navy, Rome
Captain: Lt. Tullio Dequal
Rig: Bermudian yawl
Colour of hull: white
Year built: 1965
Tonnage: 62 tons Thames
Length over all: 21,46 m.; 70.4 ft.
Length of hull: 21,46 m.; 70.4 ft.
Beam: 4,90 m.; 16.1 ft.
Draft: 3,01 m.; 9.9 ft.

Sail area: 450 qm.; 4844 sq. ft.
Auxiliary motor: 120 HP
Permanent crew: 6, including 3 officers
Cadets: 9
Took part in: Spithead–The Skaw
Sail number: 4519

Susaleen

Country: Finland

Swantewid

Country: Poland
Owner: Polskiklub Morski, Danzig
Captain: Gerzy Pettke
Rig: Bermudian cutter
Tonnage: 12 tons Thames
Length over all: 15,94 m.; 52.3 ft.
Length of hull: 13,24 m.; 43.4 ft.
Beam: 3,30 m.; 10.9 ft.
Draft: 2,30 m.; 7.5 ft.
Permanent crew: 1
Cadets: 9

Te Vega
ex Etak

Country: Panama
Owner: De Flint School, Gouda, Holland
Captain: Cpt. James M. Stoll
Rig: gaff schooner
Colour of hull: blue
Year built: 1932
Builders: Germania Shipyard, Kiel
Tonnage: 380 tons Thames
Length over all: 46,32 m.; 152 ft.
Length of hull: 40,84 m.; 134 ft.
Beam: 8,53 m.; 28 ft.
Draft: 5,12 m.; 16.8 ft.
Sail area: 700 qm.; 7535 sq. ft.
Auxiliary motor: 105 HP
Permanent crew: 10 officers
Cadets: 30
Took part in: Helsinki–Falsterbo
Sail number: TS
35

Urania
ex Tromp

Country: Holland
Owner: Royal Dutch Navy, Den Helder
Captain: Cdr. G. Jungslager
Rig: Bermudian ketch
Colour of hull: white
Year built: 1928
Builder: Haarlem Scheepsbouw Mij.,
Haarlem

Tonnage: 85 tons Thames
Length over all: 23,75 m.; 78 ft.
Length of hull: 19,00 m.; 62.3 ft.
Beam: 5,50 m.; 18 ft.
Draft: 3,20 m.; 10.5 ft.
Sail area: 763 qm.; 8213 sq. ft.

Westward Ho

Country: Faroes (Denmark)
Owner: Grunnurin "Sluppin" Thorshavn
Captain: Debes Christiansen
Rig: gaff ketch
Tonnage: 173 tons Thames
Length over all: 32,00 m.; 105 ft.
Length of hull: 25,90 m.; 85 ft.
Beam: 6,40 m.; 21 ft.
Draft: 3,23 m.; 10.6 ft.
Sail number: TS
D 42

Zawosza Czarny

Country: Poland
Owner: Zwiazek-Harcerstwa Polskiego,
Kolberg
Captain: Leonard Sadlowski
Rig: three-masted staysail schooner
Colour of hull: white
Year built: 1952
Builder: Stcznia Polnocna, Danzig
Tonnage: 197 tons Thames
Length over all: 42,67 m.; 140 ft.
Length of hull: 35,96 m.; 118 ft.
Beam: 6,70 m.; 22 ft.
Draft: 4,27 m.; 14 ft.
Sail area: 550 qm.; 5920 sq. ft.
Auxiliary motor: 300 HP
Permanent crew: 20, including 4 officers
Cadets: 25
Took part in: Helsinki–Falsterbo
Sail number: XXXX
PZ-1

Zenobe Gramme

Country: Belgium
Owner: Belgian Navy, Brussels
Captain: Lt. Barbieux
Rig: Bermudian ketch
Colour of hull: white
Year built: 1961
Tonnage: 161 tons Thames
Length over all: 28,19 m.; 92.5 ft.
Length of hull: 28,19 m.; 92.5 ft.
Beam: 6,85 m.; 22.5 ft.
Draft: 2,62 m.; 8.6 ft.

Sail area: 240 qm.; 2583 sq. ft.
Auxiliary motor: 200 HP
Permanent crew: 7, including 2 officers
Cadets: 9
Took part in: Spithead–The Skaw
Sail number: TS
B 39

Zulu

Country: Great Britain
Owner: B. A. Stewart, London
Captain: B. A. Stewart
Rig: Bermudian sloop
Colour of hull: white
Year built: 1955/6
Builder: Morris & Lorimer, Ltd.
Designer: Laurent Giles & Partners
Tonnage: 19 tons Thames
Length over all: 14,50 m.; 47.6 ft.
Length of hull: 14,50 m.; 47.6 ft.
Beam: 3,41 m.; 11.1 ft.
Draft: 2,28 m.; 7.5 ft.
Permanent crew: 3 officers
Cadets: 5
Took part in: Spithead–The Skaw
Sail number: 1034